YOUR PASSPORT TO GREECE

by Golriz Golkar

CAPSTONE PRESS
a capstone imprint

Published by Capstone Press, an imprint of Capstone
1710 Roe Crest Drive, North Mankato, Minnesota 56003
capstonepub.com

Copyright © 2025 by Capstone. All rights reserved. No part of this publication may be reproduced in whole or in part, or stored in a retrieval system, or transmitted in any form or by any means, electronic, mechanical, photocopying, recording, or otherwise, without written permission of the publisher.

Library of Congress Cataloging-in-Publication Data is available on the Library of Congress website.
ISBN: 9781669087281 (hardcover)
ISBN: 9781669087236 (paperback)
ISBN: 9781669087243 (ebook PDF)

Summary: What is it like to live in or visit Greece? What makes Greece's culture unique? Explore the geography, traditions, and daily lives of Greeks.

Editorial Credits
Editor: Carrie Sheely; Designer: Elyse White; Media Researcher: Jo Miller; Production Specialist: Tori Abraham

Image Credits
Alamy: Album, 14, Heritage Image Partnership Ltd , 11 (bottom), Luigi Girola, 19; Eric Gohl, 5; Getty Images: Carol Yepes, 29, George Pachantouris, 13, PeopleImages, 6, ZU_09, 9; Shutterstock: Aerial-motion, 17, Andreas Wolochow, 11 (top), Andrew Mayovskyy, 7, Georgios Tsichlis, 25, Gil C, cover (flag), gorwol, 26, Kirk Fisher, 21, ph.FAB, 27, SnapFocus, 22, stas11, cover (map outline), Sven Hansche, 18, Tomas Marek, cover (bottom), Victoria Kurylo, 12

Design Elements
Getty Images: Yevhenii Dubinko; Shutterstock, Flipser, Net Vector, pingebat

Any additional websites and resources referenced in this book are not maintained, authorized, or sponsored by Capstone. All product and company names are trademarks™ or registered® trademarks of their respective holders.

Printed and bound in China. 6098

CONTENTS

CHAPTER ONE
WELCOME TO GREECE! 4

CHAPTER TWO
HISTORY OF GREECE 8

CHAPTER THREE
EXPLORE GREECE 16

CHAPTER FOUR
DAILY LIFE 20

CHAPTER FIVE
HOLIDAYS AND CELEBRATIONS 24

CHAPTER SIX
SPORTS AND RECREATION 26

GLOSSARY 30
READ MORE 31
INTERNET SITES 31
INDEX 32

Words in **bold** are in the glossary.

CHAPTER ONE

WELCOME TO GREECE!

The sun rises on the island of Corfu in Greece. Olive and lemon trees dot the land. Blue waves crash against pebbly beaches. In towns, the smell of grilled lamb drifts from restaurants. Visitors stroll past old churches and palaces. Their designs show the island's Venetian, French, and British past. Greece is a country with a rich **culture**.

Greece is located in southeastern Europe. The mainland is mostly mountainous. Lowland valleys divide mountain ranges. Thousands of islands surround the mainland. Sandy beaches run along the coastlines.

The **climate** in Greece is mainly mild. Summers are dry and hot. Winters are mild and wet. Snow falls in mountainous areas in winter.

Explore Greece's cities and landmarks.

FACT

About 75 percent of Greece is mountainous. The country is one of the most mountainous in Europe.

5

THE GREEK PEOPLE

More than 10 million people live in Greece. Greek is the official language. Almost all Greek citizens have Greek roots. There are also small groups of Greek citizens with Albanian, Macedonian, Turkish, or other backgrounds. Greek is the official language of Greece. Many Greeks speak more than one language, and English is commonly spoken.

Time with family members is important for many Greeks.

FACT FILE

OFFICIAL NAME: HELLENIC REPUBLIC
POPULATION: 10,497,595
LAND AREA: 50,444 SQ. MI. (130,649 SQ KM)
CAPITAL: ATHENS
MONEY: EURO
GOVERNMENT: PARLIAMENTARY REPUBLIC
LANGUAGE: GREEK
GEOGRAPHY: Greece is located in southeastern Europe. It borders Albania, North Macedonia, and Bulgaria to the north, Turkey and the Aegean Sea to the east, the Mediterranean Sea to the south, and the Ionian Sea to the west.
NATURAL RESOURCES: petroleum, coal, bauxite, silver, marble, olives, corn

Corfu, Greece

CHAPTER TWO

HISTORY OF GREECE

Greece is home to one of the world's oldest **civilizations**. The first people to live there were the Minoans. They came from the region that is now Turkey. They arrived on the island of Crete around 2600 BCE. The Minoans were known for their writing and building designs. About 2000 BCE, the Mycenaeans came to mainland Greece. The Mycenaeans had a strong army.

The Minoans disappeared by 1500 BCE. Some historians think a volcanic eruption caused a **tsunami** that led to their downfall. Others think the Mycenaeans may have defeated them.

By 1100 BCE, most of the Mycenaeans had disappeared from Greece. The Dorians settled in western Greece. Those who settled in eastern Greece were called Ionians. The Dorians and Ionians made new buildings. Markets and community meeting places appeared.

By 1000 BCE, **city-states** had formed. They had their own governments and armies. Athens and Sparta were powerful city-states. Together, they drove out Persian invaders.

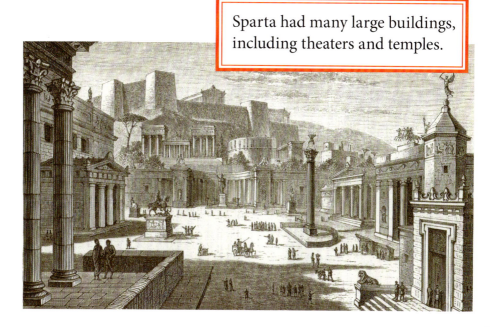

Sparta had many large buildings, including theaters and temples.

FAMOUS ANCIENT GREEKS

Several ancient Greeks made important accomplishments. Socrates was a great thinker and teacher. Pythagoras was an important mathematician. Hippocrates was a doctor. He healed many people and wrote about his treatments.

A THRIVING CULTURE

Over the next 500 years, the Greek civilization thrived. The Greeks built a major library. Greece became a hub for literature, science, art, and **philosophy**. In 776 BCE, the first Olympic Games were held in southern Greece. Events included sprinting, jumping, and wrestling.

In the early 500s BCE, Athens formed a government that involved citizens. Free adult male citizens could vote. They also helped make laws. This system influenced today's **democratic** governments. Athens is sometimes called the birthplace of democracy.

ALEXANDER THE GREAT

In 336 BCE, Alexander the Great came to power. He came from Macedon, a kingdom north of Greece. He unified the Greek city-states. Greek culture spread throughout his large empire. In 323 BCE, Alexander the Great died. His generals fought one another for power.

A piece of artwork from the 100s BCE showed Alexander the Great on a horse in battle.

FACT

Ancient Greeks worshipped many gods and goddesses, including Zeus and Hera. These figures were believed to be heroes or protectors of Greek life. Stories from Greek **mythology** are well known.

ROMAN RULE

In 146 BCE, the Roman Empire took over Greece. City-states continued to rule. The Roman Empire expanded. In 324 CE, it divided in two. The eastern half was called Greek Byzantium. The Romans adopted many Greek ideas and traditions. In 410, German invaders took over the western empire.

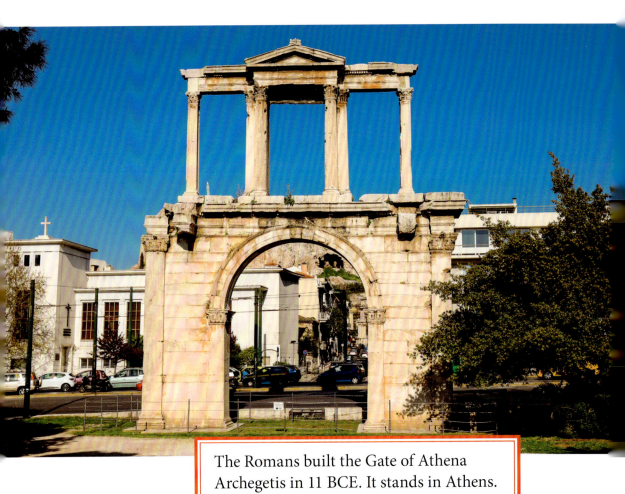

The Romans built the Gate of Athena Archegetis in 11 BCE. It stands in Athens.

From the 1100s to around 1800, the Venetian Republic also controlled parts of Greece. They were from modern-day northeastern Italy.

In 1453, the Ottoman Empire conquered Greek Byzantium. It ruled this region for nearly 400 years. The Ottomans fought many wars with the Republic of Venice.

FACT
Romans used some of the Greeks' building and sculpture styles. These included the use of columns.

MODERN GREECE

The Ottomans were Muslim, and most Greeks were not. This caused problems for many Greeks. Non-Muslim Greeks often had to pay taxes or send their sons to become soldiers. Many Greeks became frustrated. They wanted to rule themselves.

In 1821, the Greeks began a long war for independence against the Ottomans. The **revolutionary** fighters won their independence in 1832. By the early 1900s, Greece had regained most of its land. The government changed many times. In 1974, Greece became a republic with its first elected president.

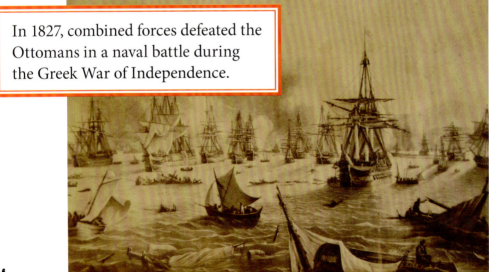

In 1827, combined forces defeated the Ottomans in a naval battle during the Greek War of Independence.

TIMELINE OF GREEK HISTORY

ABOUT 2600 BCE: The Minoans arrive in Greece.

ABOUT 2000 BCE: The Mycenaeans arrive in Greece.

1100 BCE: The Mycenaeans disappear from Greece. Dorians settle in western Greece, while Ionians settle in eastern Greece.

ABOUT 1000 BCE: City-states are in Greece.

776 BCE: The first Olympic Games are held in Olympia, Greece.

336 BCE: Alexander the Great comes to power in Greece.

323 BCE: Alexander the Great dies, leaving local generals to fight for power over Greece.

146 BCE: The Roman Empire conquers Greece, ruling for hundreds of years.

324 CE: The eastern half of the Roman Empire becomes Greek Byzantium.

ABOUT 1100: The Venetian Republic governs some Greek islands.

1453: The Ottoman Empire overthrows the Romans and takes over Greek Byzantium.

1832: Greece wins its independence from the Ottoman Empire.

1974: Greece becomes a republic with its first elected president.

2009: Greece experiences an economic debt crisis.

2018: With support from European countries, Greece improves its economy.

In recent times, Greece has had problems with neighboring countries over land. Some Greeks have had trouble getting jobs. But Greek life has been slowly improving. **Treaties** have restored peace with neighbors, and the economy is rebounding.

CHAPTER THREE
EXPLORE GREECE

Greece offers beautiful islands, vibrant cities, and wondrous ancient sites. These places give visitors a look at the country's modern life and distant past.

MODERN CITIES

Athens is the capital of Greece. It is on the mainland. Visitors can buy traditional foods at the Athens Central Market. They can have picnics on the Hill of the Muses where an ancient Roman monument still stands. There are also museums to visit. The National Archaeological Museum displays Greek **artifacts**. The National Museum of Contemporary Art shows modern paintings.

Thessaloniki is Greece's second-largest city. Like Athens, it has many historical sites. A large statue honors Alexander the Great.

The National Archaeological Museum sits in the heart of Athens.

Kalamata is a lively port city. Visitors can go horseback riding on the beach. They can taste local Kalamata olives at a market. The Kalamata Castle is a popular attraction. It was used by nearly every civilization that ruled Greece. It offers sweeping city views.

ANCIENT SITES

Greece has many ancient sites. The Acropolis is a group of white marble buildings on a hill in Athens. Many of its buildings were built more than 1,500 years ago. It contains many temples. The Parthenon and others were built to honor ancient Greek gods and goddesses. Ancient Olympia has ruins of structures that were set up for the first Olympic Games. The Temple of Apollo in Delphi was a religious site.

The Acropolis is easily visible among its flatter surroundings.

BEAUTIFUL ISLANDS

Greece has many islands. Crete is the largest. It has sandy beaches, turquoise waters, and palm forests. Visitors can see Minoan palaces. Santorini is known for its white buildings with blue domes. Some of its beaches have black sand produced by material from volcanoes.

NATIONAL PARKS

Many people enjoy visiting Greece's national parks. Mount Olympus National Park has 52 mountain peaks. Roe deer, chamois, and jackals roam the land. The peregrine falcon, booted eagle, and sparrow hawk fly through the sky. Samaria National Park is home to about 450 plant **species** as well as many animals. The kri-kri goat is native to the park. Cretan wildcats and bearded vultures also live there.

Kri-kri goats

CHAPTER FOUR
DAILY LIFE

Four out of five Greeks live in and around cities such as Athens. Stone is a common building material for houses. Buses, cars, and trains provide transportation in urban areas. Ferries take people between islands.

A small number of Greeks live in rural or island areas. They may walk or ride donkeys to get around.

Many Greeks work in small shops or in tourism. Fishing is another common industry. A small number of Greeks work on farms. Farmers may grow olives and fruits or raise animals.

Most Greeks belong to the Greek Orthodox church. Others are Muslim, Jewish, Catholic, or Protestant. Religion is important in the daily lives of many Greeks.

TRADITIONS AND FAMILY

Family is very important in Greek culture. Grandparents often live with or near their children. Families celebrate holidays and important events together.

Most Greeks wear modern clothing. In some island or rural areas, traditional clothing is worn. On Crete, men may wear high boots, breeches, and tasseled handkerchiefs. Women may wear long shirts, pants, and aprons.

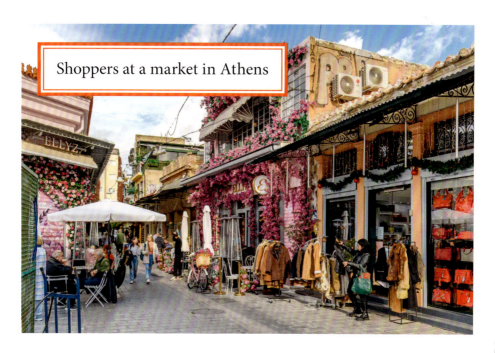

Shoppers at a market in Athens

FOOD

Greek meals often feature olive oil, fish, meat, and vegetables. Breakfast may include bread, butter, and jam or yogurt with honey. Meats such as lamb and chicken may be part of lunch. Souvlaki is chunky meat served with tomatoes, onions, and yogurt sauce wrapped in pita bread. Dinners may include the national dish of moussaka. Eggplant layers are mixed with spicy beef and vegetables.

For dessert, pastries or custard pies are common. People enjoy cookies on holidays or for special events.

Moussaka

KOURABIEDES

Kourabiedes are shortbread cookies often served on Greek holidays. You will need an adult's help to make them.

Ingredients:
- 1¼ cups butter
- 1¼ cups powdered sugar
- 2½ cups flour
- ½ teaspoon baking powder
- 1 teaspoon vanilla extract
- ¾ cup crushed almonds

Directions:
1. Preheat oven to 310°F (154°C).
2. Put the butter and ¾ of the powdered sugar in a large mixing bowl. Save the rest of the sugar for dusting.
3. Cream the sugar and butter. Slowly add in the flour, baking powder, and vanilla. Combine the ingredients well to form a dough.
4. Ask an adult to help you crush the almonds into medium-sized pieces with a food processor or rolling pin. You may also use pre-crushed almonds.
5. Fold them into the dough.
6. Using a tablespoon, divide the dough into tablespoon-sized pieces. With your hands, make each one into a ball shape.
7. Place the dough balls a few centimeters apart on a lined baking sheet. Chill the sheet in the refrigerator for one hour.
8. Bake the cookies for 25 minutes. They should look golden.
9. Remove the cookies from the oven and let them cool.
10. Using a sifter, sprinkle the remaining powdered sugar over the cookies.

CHAPTER FIVE
HOLIDAYS AND CELEBRATIONS

Greeks enjoy celebrations and holidays. Carnival is celebrated before Greek Orthodox Easter. For about three weeks, people dance, play music, have parades, and feast together. Many wear masks and costumes.

Most Greeks celebrate Greek Orthodox Easter. People attend church and eat special foods such as roasted lamb. Fireworks and parades are common.

Christmas is an important holiday for most Greeks. Before Christmas, families bake cookies. Seaside residents decorate boats with lights. Celebrations begin on December 24 and last for about two weeks. During this period, families enjoy feasts. They sing carols and go to church.

NATIONAL HOLIDAYS

Greeks celebrate Greek Independence Day on March 25. It marks the day the country declared war against the Ottomans. Military parades are held all over Greece.

Labor Day is celebrated on May 1. Shops, markets, and transportation close down. Many people picnic in the countryside.

Fireworks light up the skies over Crete to celebrate Greek Orthodox Easter.

NAME DAYS

Name days are celebrated in Greece. They are days when the Greek Orthodox Church celebrates a certain saint. Anyone who shares a name with that saint also celebrates. Family and friends visit that person's house. They offer small gifts and share a meal.

CHAPTER SIX
SPORTS AND RECREATION

Dance is an important part of Greek culture. One popular dance is the sirtaki. People stand in a line or a circle. They place their hands on the shoulders of those next to them. They start a slow dance to Greek traditional music that becomes faster. It is often danced at weddings. The kalamatianos is one of the most famous Greek dances. Dancers hold hands and dance in a circle. It is often danced at festivals and other celebrations.

People dance the sirtaki at a festival.

The national sport is soccer. Many people enjoy watching and playing it. The national men's team has played in European and World Cup games.

FACT

In 2004, the men's national soccer team from Greece won the European Championship. Celebrations were held all over Greece.

ABARIZA

Abariza is a game in Greece that children have played since ancient times.

1. Form two teams with three or more players per team.
2. In a large field or on a blacktop surface, draw a long line to separate the teams using chalk or a stick in the dirt. The teams can be called Team A and B.
3. On each side of the line, each team must draw a large circle. This is the team's hideout. About 30 feet (10 meters) from the hideout, each team should draw a large square that is about 13 feet (4 m) on each side. This is the team's prison.
4. The players all stand inside their team's hideout. Each team chooses a player to do the first run. On the count of three, both players run toward each other, crossing the line. Each tries to tag the other first.
5. The player who is tagged first goes to the prison of the other team.
6. The next two players from opposite teams do their run. From this point forward, each player can try to release any teammates in prison by tapping them during their tag run. Released players go back to their team's hideout.
7. The team that puts all of the other team's players in prison first wins the game.

Other activities are popular. People enjoy hiking, climbing, and skiing in the mountains. Water sports include swimming, scuba diving, and boating. People enjoy playing basketball. The national basketball team has won European championships. Gymnastics and track and field events are popular as well.

PAST AND PRESENT

Greeks have a long history of rich culture and great accomplishments. From ancient sites and mythology to bustling cities, Greece is a country where the past meets the present.

The remains of the Temple of Olympian Zeus (center) in Athens are a reminder of Greece's past. It was completed in the early 100s CE.

29

GLOSSARY

artifact (AR-tuh-fakt)
an object used in the past that was made by people

city-state (SI-tee-STAYT)
a self-governing community including a town and its surroundings

civilization (si-vuh-ly-ZAY-shuhn)
a highly developed and organized society

climate (KLY-muht)
the usual weather that occurs in a place

culture (KUHL-chuhr)
a people's way of life, ideas, art, customs, and traditions

democratic (de-muh-KRA-tik)
related to a kind of government in which citizens vote for their leaders

mythology (mi-THOL-uh-jee)
old or ancient stories

philosophy (fuh-LOSS-uh-fee)
the study of ideas, the way people think, and the search for knowledge

revolutionary (rev-uh-LOO-shun-air-ee)
involving an uprising by a group of people against a system of government or a way of life

species (SPEE-sheez)
a group of plants or animals that share common characteristics

tsunami (tsoo-NAH-mee)
a very large wave

READ MORE

Leaf, Christina. *Greece*. Minneapolis: Bellwether Media, Inc., 2020.

Lukidis, Lydia. *Zeus vs. Ra: Clash of the Gods*. North Mankato, MN: Capstone, 2023.

Peters, Stephanie. *Jason and the Argonauts: A Modern Graphic Greek Myth*. North Mankato, MN: Capstone, 2024.

INTERNET SITES

BBC Bitesize: The History of the Olympic Games
bbc.co.uk/bitesize/topics/z87tn39/articles/z4q3bqt#zdd8dp3

National Geographic Kids: Greece
kids.nationalgeographic.com/geography/countries/article/greece

National Geographic Kids: The Gods and Goddesses of Ancient Greece!
natgeokids.com/ie/discover/history/greece/greek-gods

INDEX

Acropolis, 18
Alexander the Great, 10, 11, 15, 16
Athens, 7, 9, 10, 12, 16, 17, 18, 20, 21, 29

beaches, 4, 17, 19

Carnival, 24
Christmas, 24
city-states, 9, 10, 12, 15
clothing, 21

dancing, 24, 26
Dorians, 8, 15

foods, 4, 16, 20, 22, 23, 24

Independence Day, 25
Ionians, 8, 15
islands, 4, 8, 13, 15, 16, 19, 20, 21

Minoans, 8, 15, 19
Mycenaeans, 8, 15
mythology, 11, 29

Olympic Games, 10, 15, 18
Ottoman Empire, 13, 14, 15, 25

Romans, 12, 13, 15, 16

soccer, 27

ABOUT THE AUTHOR

Golriz Golkar is the author of more than 70 books for children. Inspired by her work as an elementary school teacher, she loves to write the kinds of books that children are excited to read. Golriz holds a B.A. in American literature and culture from UCLA and a master's degree in education from the Harvard Graduate School of Education. Golriz lives in France with her husband and young daughter, and they all love reading together.

SELECT BOOKS IN THIS SERIES

YOUR PASSPORT TO AUSTRALIA
YOUR PASSPORT TO BRAZIL
YOUR PASSPORT TO CUBA
YOUR PASSPORT TO EGYPT
YOUR PASSPORT TO ENGLAND
YOUR PASSPORT TO GERMANY
YOUR PASSPORT TO JAPAN
YOUR PASSPORT TO MEXICO
YOUR PASSPORT TO PORTUGAL
YOUR PASSPORT TO SAUDI ARABIA